Zuñi olla with "Rain Bird" design.

Pueblo Designs

176 ILLUSTRATIONS OF THE "RAIN BIRD"

H. P. MERA

Drawings by Tom Lea

DOVER PUBLICATIONS, INC.
NEW YORK

Published in Canada by General Publishing Com-
pany, Ltd., 30 Lesmill Road, Don Mills, Toronto,
Ontario.
Published in the United Kingdom by Constable
and Company, Ltd., 10 Orange Street, London
WC 2.

This Dover edition, first published in 1970, is an
unabridged republication of the work originally
published by the Laboratory of Anthropology, Santa
Fe, New Mexico, in 1937 as Volume II of their
series of Memoirs, with the title *"The Rain Bird":
A Study in Pueblo Design*. The present edition is
published by special arrangement with the School
of American Research in Santa Fe.

International Standard Book Number: 0-486-22073-7
Library of Congress Catalog Card Number: 73-127847

Manufactured in the United States of America
Dover Publications, Inc.
180 Varick Street
New York, N.Y. 10014

CONTENTS

PLATES

FOREWORD

THE following monograph should by no means be viewed as an exhaustive treatise, for the space required for such an undertaking would far exceed that deemed sufficient for the present need; nor, the writer believes, would greater clarity be achieved by the mere piling up of a multiplicity of illustrative material. In fact, it has been somewhat difficult at times to avoid the inclusion of interesting unessentials and pursue an undeviating course as there were so many intriguing, interdigitating factors involving paralleling design developments which constantly obtruded during the progress of study. Although developmental progression has received considerable attention, yet the underlying motive in the preparation of this paper has been the hope of stimulating an interest in indigenous American art-forms as source material for a future system of decoration—one that undoubtedly can be made to possess both a pleasing and highly distinctive character.

Finally, the author wishes to make grateful acknowledgement to the American Council of Learned Societies for the funds provided, by which a presentation of this thesis in published form has been made possible.

H. P. M.

"RAIN BIRD"

UPON viewing, for the first time, a large collection of Pueblo pottery of the historic period gathered from the various villages where the art of the potter has been perpetuated for the last three centuries, one is very likely to be impressed by the seemingly endless variety of design. A more critical study, however, discloses the fact that in reality astonishingly few basic elements were employed to produce complex design structures; also that simple basic elements through elaboration often become what may be termed design units, so that these, too, may be used in combination. To illustrate this, it is the object of this paper to make an analysis of a well known and frequently used design occurring on Zuñi water jars, which, according to popular usage, is known as the "Rain Bird". By what right the term is used or where it originated is unknown to the writer, but it may serve to designate this formalized design which seems to mark the culmination of one developmental series and the point of departure for another. An effort will be made to demonstrate its probable origin through the basic elements from which it was derived as well as to show the numerous later forms resulting from modification of the original concept. That many of these variations of the original were very popular over the Pueblo area is evidenced by the fact that there is not a pottery-making pueblo producing the decorated wares of the historic period, except perhaps the pueblos of Jemez and Pecos, which did not adopt some form of this design or incorporate portions of it with its own decorative system.

In tracing the ancestry of the "Rain Bird" design, it will be necessary to go back to the very beginnings of decorated pottery in the Southwest—to a ceramic type which as reckoned by present day archaeologists, came into existence some time during the early centuries of the Christian era. At this stage decoration was in a very rudimentary state and consisted largely of crudely drawn lines and dots with little attempt at organization (Pl. I, 1). This period is known as Basket Maker III because it has been determined that, although pottery had begun to replace basketry for some purposes, the latter remained the dominant art having been carried over from the preceding exclusively basket-making periods, I and II.

As time went on and Basket Maker pottery styles began a gradual transition into those of the next period, Pueblo I, the result of an infiltration of an alien people, it will be seen that there was an effort to effect a semblance of order. Dots heretofore scattered almost at random are now found arranged in rows, placed parallel to lines or appended to them (Pl. I, 2-3). It is also apparent that some

---

NOTE: The designs used to illustrate the following discussion were copied from vessels or their fragments selected from the collection of the Indian Arts Fund, Laboratory of Anthropology, and a few from other sources, for which credit is given, and their catalogue or site numbers appended.

of the dots have become elongate or even prolonged into short lines to form a sort of fringe at right angles to a principal structural line.

The next step in development to be considered consisted of the introduction of a solid mass into design construction. This is a distinctly new feature as previously patterns were evolved merely from different arrangements of lines and dots. A decided change in the character of design was produced by filling in the angle between one side of a fringe element and the base line (Pl. I, 4). It also may be noted in passing, though of no especial concern with the subject in hand, that this procedure accounts for the origin of the widely used pendant triangle as well.

By representing the distal ends of fringe elements as bent, a hook was achieved which could be angled or curved, (Pl. I, 5), and when two of these were placed opposite each other in such a manner that the hooks engaged, the simplest form of perhaps the most widely used design unit in Southwestern pottery was produced (Pl. I, 6). Hook elements were used not only in series but singly as well. The writer makes no claim that all such interlocking coils or frets, wherever found, were evolved in the manner described but it can be seen that there is an apparently unbroken succession of developmental steps throughout several of the earlier archæological horizons of the Pueblo region.

It should not be assumed that as designs became more complex and elaborate the older and simpler forms were discarded. On the contrary, even such a primitive feature as the line with pendant dots was retained and carried on through various cultural periods to the present.

On Plate II, 1-6, drawings are shown illustrating a few of the multifarious forms assumed by the design unit, the development of which has just been postulated.

The final step in elaboration consists in differentiating one of the interlocking members from the other. This was accomplished by opposing hatched and solid elements (Pl. II, 7).

Hitherto, the discussion has outlined a development general over a wide area in northern Arizona and New Mexico. It is now necessary to restrict this to a specialized form of interlocking coil found in a cultural phase, one of the many later specializations, as it is from this source that the so-called "Rain Bird" was largely derived. The area in which this standardized feature occurs, though not as yet definitely defined, may be said broadly to embrace a considerable scope of country in east central Arizona and adjoining tracts in New Mexico. The latest black-on-white pottery type found in this region has been named Tularosa Black-on-white[*] and differs from other wares of its period by the very frequent use of specialized and standardized forms of interlocking design units (Pl. III, 1-2). Haury[†] has given a date of circa 1290 for the height of development of a western marginal variety of

---

* Gladwin, W. and H. S.; 1931, pp. 32-35.
† Haury, E. W.; 1931, p. 74.

this black-on-white pottery which used a similar system of design. His date, there-fore, will probably apply in a general way to the whole Tularosa area. When the popularity of black-on-white pottery was on the wane, due to the introduction of a decorated red ware which was in part contemporaneous with but finally replaced it entirely, the characteristic Tularosa designs were retained for a while on the red ware. At first decoration was applied to this new type with a paint possessing a matte surface but which was in time supplanted by one that fired to a glaze. During the glaze-paint period, especially in the latter part, designs are seen to have largely broken away from the Tularosa system and, so far as the writer has been able to determine, the elaborate interlocking patterns of the matte paint series are less in evidence during most of the time that glaze paint was in vogue. An important fact should here be noted; that as yet there had been no attempt to connect, in the Tularosa region, the idea of a bird with any part of the purely geometric progression just outlined but as the bird concept is shown so plainly in the Zuñi design that forms the subject of this article, it is obvious that search must be made elsewhere for graphic forms connecting the two.

Zoomorphic figures with undoubtedly avian-like characteristics, (Pl. IV, 4-5), are not rare on Mesa Verde Black-on-white pottery—the product of a distinct cultural group in a part of the Pueblo region considerably removed to the north from close contact with the peoples of the Tularosa group. Cutting dates for beams secured from pueblos, when calculated by the Douglass tree-ring method, indicate that Mesa Verde pottery had reached a peak of excellence sometime during the 13th Century. Bird-like figures are frequently found on pottery of this classical period, thus postulating their use at a time when the Tularosa type was still restricted almost entirely to the geometric.

Although somewhat aside from the present concern, the writer believes that these bird forms were the result, in the first place, of a fortuitous arrangement of a basic coil and an elaboration of its appendages which suggested the later applica-tion (Pl. IV, 1-2-3).

The Mesa Verde graphic bird motif in time spread to adjacent regions where it was adopted with little or no change in style. Attention is now called to its frequent use on a yellow ware, Jeddito Black-on-yellow*, which appeared on a time horizon believed to be somewhat later than that of Mesa Verde. It is inter-esting to note that when interlocking design units were used in the Jeddito type they were of a simple and elementary sort, in no way approaching the specialized forms developed in the Tularosa region. Having briefly mentioned the adoption of a bird figure on this later pottery type (Pl. IV, 6-7) the matter will be dropped for the present to be again considered when pertinent to the discussion.

Returning to the area on the western periphery of the Tularosa region, men-tioned before as having been investigated by Haury†, it is known that bird forms similar to those of the Mesa Verde culture had been introduced on the latest black-

* Hargrave, L. L.; 1932, p. 29.
† Haury, E. W.; op. cit.

on-white wares of this peripheral section and further that they also appeared on a red ware which succeeded it—Four-mile Polychrome (Pl. IV, 8-9), but the use of these figures, however, seems to have been largely confined to the outsides of bowls.

As Four-mile Polychrome followed shortly after a pottery type closely akin to Tularosa Black-on-white, in which the purely geometric interlocking coil was much in evidence, it is not surprising to find some features of this pattern surviving. The Four-mile period may be generalized as one possessing great exuberance of decoration in which a black glaze paint bordered by narrow white lines was used. In this pottery type only a single element of the ancestral interlocking design unit was retained with the plain background of the bowl acting as a foil to bring it into prominence (Pl. V, 1-4).

According to recognized authorities, Four-mile Polychrome pottery was contemporaneous with the Jeddito Black-on-yellow type which has been previously mentioned as using bird symbols. Also significant is the fact that many villages situated along the border between the two cultures exhibit considerable quantities of both pottery types, all of which argues for a close association with ample opportunity for an exchange of ideas.

Haury* ventures the opinion that Four-mile Polychrome may have survived until the beginning of the 15th Century after which it seems to have disappeared but the Hopi yellow wares, of which Jeddito Black-on-yellow is a component, have persisted through several decorative periods to the present day. In one of these, Sikyatki Polychrome which immediately followed the Jeddito type and which reached its height shortly before the coming of the Spanish, may be seen the fruits of a fusion of the Jeddito bird concept with that of the Four-mile Polychrome single coil element. This fusion of ideas appears to have brought about those fantastically elaborate figures, recognized by Fewkes† as highly conventionalized bird forms (Pl. VI, 1-2), which were characteristic of a remarkable system of abstract design.

Sikyatki-type pottery became very popular over the whole Pueblo region of that period. Sherds of this ware are found in the refuse heaps of villages at great distances from the center of its distribution. The six Zuñi towns, nearest neighbors of the Hopi during the 16th Century, were well acquainted with yellow ware designs and were influenced by them to some extent, as were the Hopi by Zuñi decoration at a subsequent period, a matter which will be taken up later.

THE PUEBLO OF ZUÑI

It has been proved, in a general way, that the people of the Tularosa culture were ancestral to those of Zuñi but notwithstanding this fact, few traces are found of a survival of typical Tularosa design, beyond the pre-glaze red-wares of that

* Haury, E. W.; op. cit. p. 77.
† Fewkes, J. W.; 1898, pp. 519-742.

region. The glaze paint, however, persisted through the years of confusion attending the efforts of the Spanish to bring the Pueblos under subjection. About the year 1700, a new type of pottery began to make its appearance in the pueblo of Zuñi, which at this time sheltered the survivors of the six original villages first discovered by the Spaniards in 1540. Glaze paint was discarded on this new ware in favor of one having a dull flat appearance—similar to the paint in use today. It is on this pottery type that the "Rain Bird" design has been first noted. The design presents a curious blending of the single coil bird concept, which is reminiscent of Sikyatki treatment, with other features derived from the old Tularosa Black-on-white system of decoration. The design is divisible into a number of distinct features. Near the center is a single coil, partly solid and partly hatched, representing a conventionalized bird's head and beak (Pl. VII, 1, *A*). Both above and below this are several elements which are thought perhaps to represent a crest (Pl. VII, 1, *B-C*), while on either side of the central section are hatched areas having a stepped outline arranged so as to include two solid figures. Taken together, these are presumed to indicate a body and wings.

It is rather astonishing that after a lapse of nearly three hundred years, the revival of Black-on-white age decoration should have been considered, unless animated by a veneration for things of the past. If such a premise be assumed and its origin be ascribed to a desire to perpetuate on ceremonial vessels an idea connected with tradition, such a restricted use did not obtain for long, as water jars of this type, for domestic use, have been continuously produced up to the present time. The author is convinced, from many years' observation, that designs originally conceived for ceremonial use may, through popular fancy and repetition, entirely lose their first significance and become mere decoration.

Upon an examination of the "Rain Bird" motif, it is quite obvious that the arrangement of hatched areas has less of the organized conventionalism of the Tularosa period but many features are preserved with so little alteration that they may be readily identified. On Plate VII the relationships between the old and the new are shown by means of letters which will be continued in use throughout the remainder of the paper when reference is made to those fundamental features designated by them. The same plate (VII, 4-5) figures, in addition, a variation from which the coil element has been omitted and an adaptation of the old pendant dot idea substituted. The omission of so important a design element plainly indicates a breaking down of the original conception.

This process of alteration will be seen to continue in various ways until finally it is sometimes hard to realize that many of the resultant end-products could be in any way related either to one another or to a common ancestral pattern. Plate VIII figures two examples in which this change, to a considerable degree, has taken place. On this same plate a design unit is shown which appears for the first time (Pl. VIII, 2, *F*). This unit becomes very important in one of the lines of later development as finally it entirely replaces the original hatched body and wing mass. On Plate XII is illustrated diagramatically the general evolutionary change which transformed this stepped figure (F) into the form later most frequently in use. Also note alterations and placement for elements B and C, which, as will be seen later, may be used or even omitted with considerable latitude of choice. In the design of which this new feature is a part, it is plain that an attempt has been made to lighten the whole structure by doing away with large hatched areas though some hatching has been retained in the three stepped appendages.

After reviewing a large number of the many mutations existing as a result of the breaking down of the original concept, it is seen that they can be separated naturally into three groups. One is composed of those designs in which a hatching of the coil element has been preserved and is the principal feature (Pls. IX, X, XI). Another, on the contrary, makes use of the solid portion of the coil only, embellished with elements B, C and the much altered rendition of design unit F (Pls. XII, XIII, XIV, XV). The third is comprised of small solid figures derived from the group last mentioned, in which the elements B and F have become coalescent with the coil element (Pl. XVI). Varieties coming within the classification of the first group are found almost exclusively on Zuñi vessels, though an occasional example may be seen from the Hopi country while, on the other hand, the two remaining groups are of the sort most esteemed for copying in other villages.

A number of Zuñi designs representative of these three groups are figured in Dr. Bunzel's study of Pueblo pottery design*. Typical examples were chosen and their various definitions as given by her several informants tabulated with interesting results. Seventeen were described as crooks; four, clouds; eight, flowers; eight, feathers, and two each as drum sticks and bows. To one unacquainted with the beliefs and manner of thinking of the Zuñi Indian there would seem to be a great diversity of ideas but when certain factors are taken into consideration there may be found grounds for definite association between them.

Without going too deeply into the subject of ceremonial symbolism, except in so far as it may influence design, it may be well to give some hint of what may possibly lie back of the mental process that can conceive closely related forms of a single design unit as representing such widely differing things as clouds, flowers and drum sticks. One explanation seems to lie in the fact that certain symbols may stand for any part of or a whole train of ideas together with their results. In order to clarify this statement, it will be necessary to call attention briefly to a few details. Crook-shaped wooden wands have been used in prehistoric times and are also employed at the present for use in ceremonies†, the purposes of which are largely connected with petitions for rain and fertility. These wands are often adorned with feathers and as there seems to have been some belief which conceived birds as prayer bearers, it may be plausible to think of the crook, and allied ceremonial objects having the same general form, as derived from a similar idea as that associated with the simple bird forms found on pottery. Zuñi drum sticks, largely used in beating drums during the singing of ritual songs, are also of this

* Bunzel, Ruth L.; 1929, Appendix I.
† Hough, Walter; 1914, pp. 93-95.

general shape, only having the end of the crook bound to the handle for more effective use. Again, miniature bows decorated with feathers are known to have been deposited as offerings in shrines devoted to ceremonial uses—no doubt, with a like end in view. With the known use of these several objects as a starting point, there can be argued a correlation between the various definitions recorded by Dr. Bunzel into a resultant composite thought of cause and effect, thus: ceremonies with their paraphernalia (crooks, drumsticks, bows and feathers) and accompanying prayers for rain; consequent gathering of clouds followed by rain; resultant new growth of vegetation typified by flowers thus signifying bounteous crops and abundant food for game. In this connection, attention is called to the drawing of a conventionalized dragonfly, one of the water symbols, copied from a ceremonial vessel, which has been conceived as having a highly abstracted form of the "Rain Bird" motif in place of the usual more or less naturalistic head (Pl. XVI, 10) and on the same plate (9) there also may be seen a bird whose tail has been formed from two of the same abstract forms.

The foregoing explanation might seem to indicate a rather active and conscious use of symbolism in designs for every day pottery but the writer has found that any consciousness of such use is principally subjective; that unless a request is made of the artist concerning a definition for a design, the idea for which it could have stood in a ceremonial sense is not actively in mind, so that generally, the only conscious use of such a design is to satisfactorily fill an allotted space.

The Zuñi "Rain Bird," in its numerous forms and at apparently various times, spread, with a few exceptions, to most of the pottery-making pueblos existing concurrently with the village in which it originated. In these, it was either adopted or adapted, often both. The first to be taken up in following the course of diffusion throughout the Pueblo area will be the Hopi towns.

THE HOPI TOWNS

It was stated, when speaking of the influence exerted by Sikyatki designs on those of the Zuñi villages during prehistoric times, that a return influence from the Zuñi to the Hopi would later be demonstrated. What actually took place at this later date should be described by a much stronger term, as the "Rain Bird" motif was adopted in its entirety, with very few important changes. The small number of added features are enough, on a more than cursory examination, to mark them as of Hopi origin. With one notable exception to the rule these adopted designs follow quite closely the stereotyped Zuñi formula. The exception shows an inventive arrangement of elements and units resulting in the formation of a distinct group of designs, examples of which are shown on Plate XX, 2-3. In these a B-C element derived from the old Tularosa system has been used as a unit separately from the coil and becomes a prominent feature, though some of the C elements not in combination are still retained in their usual position in relation to the coil. This last element, usually assuming an important place, becomes subordinate.

It is curious that the Hopi people possessing a distinct linguistic and cultural heritage, one which resulted in a measure of artistic achievement of as high an order as was displayed on Sikyatki pottery, should have been content to take over the formalized designs of the Zuñi, so much at variance with their own tradition.

ACOMA

The pueblo of Acoma lies southeast of Zuñi at a distance of nearly eighty miles in an air line. The language spoken by its inhabitants is a dialect of the Keres tongue which differs as radically from the speech of the Zuñi as does that of the Shoshonean Hopi, but ceramically, the culture of Acoma, during some of its prehistoric phases, varied little from that of its western neighbor. Though somewhat different during the late Black-on-white period, both regions were included in the territory in which the red ware with glaze paint decoration, mentioned previously, was the principal type. Due to the limitations imposed by the use of the glaze, little difference is noticeable in the system of design in use over the whole area. Later both discarded the glaze medium at about the same time in favor of a matte paint which allowed a much greater freedom of expression. It was at this latter period that Acoma began to exhibit that versatility in design for which it has since been noted. Though the "Rain Bird" motif was soon adopted, there seems to have been no attempt merely to copy but on the contrary, it appears that from the beginning only the idea was taken, to be then translated into Acoman terms. At first patterns were comparatively simple but later became more involved, finally resulting in the decadent and complex all-over decoration of the 20th Century. From the beginning of the historic period up to the present there has been a constant tendency to draw away from the strictly formal and geometric. Outside of the effort to replace angles with curves whenever possible, one other feature deserves especial mention, that of substituting stepped design units for the more conventional adaptations of the Zuñi unit F (Pl. XXI, 1).

LAGUNA

Historical records indicate that Laguna was founded by missionaries about the year 1699 as a place where proselytes could be congregated, probably in an effort to consolidate gains accomplished during the attempts to Christianize the various peoples of the Pueblo region. It is stated that converts were sent here from the Hopi towns, Zuñi and a number of the Rio Grande pueblos, so that there is a considerable mixture represented in the present day population. However, the nucleus must have been largely from Acoma as that dialect is the only aboriginal language in use at present. Further, the ceramic culture is practically identical with that of this same village which lies only a short distance to the southwest. So closely related are the ceramic products of Laguna and Acoma that it is next to impossible, without having a hint as to its origin, to tell to which village a given piece of pottery may be ascribed. As Laguna pottery is so like that of its progenitor, it has seemed best to figure only two well authenticated examples wherein the "Rain Bird" concept has been used. One, in make up, is indistinguishable from those found on Acoma pottery (Pl. XXVIII, 2); the other, which has been included for its singular beauty of arrangement is, to a large extent, a direct copy from the Zuñi with the addition of leaf-like forms of local derivation (Pl. XXVIII, 1).

THE PUEBLOS OF THE RIO GRANDE

Leaving Laguna and proceeding toward the east a group of twelve villages is encountered, grouped collectively under the name of Rio Grande pueblos. All are situated in or near the valley of the river having the same name. There were originally, previous to the year 1700, a larger number existing in this region but these were too early to have been influenced by the design which forms the subject of this paper. After the passing of the pottery types holding over from prehistoric times, which occurred at the beginning of the 18th Century, six of the twelve remaining towns are not known to have made decorated pottery, being content to produce only plain polished red and black wares. This leaves an equal number to consider as coming within the scope of this article. It may be well to explain at this time that the decorated vessels now made at Isleta are not, strictly speaking, a product of that village but are the work of a small band of Laguna people who left their homes after some disagreement and settled on the outskirts of that Rio Grande town. The design system follows closely that of Laguna and Acoma.

TSIA

The first of this group to be discussed is Tsia*. This pueblo, like Zuñi, is the sole survivor of a cluster of villages which Espejo, one of the early Spanish explorers, gave as five in number. It is situated on the Jemez River about fifteen miles above the junction of that stream with the Rio Grande. The language spoken is related to that of Acoma being a Keresan dialect but on the other hand its ceramic culture is quite different during the historic period as well as in prehistoric times. The late black-on-white pottery phase of this region was distinct from that of the western varieties previously described as occurring in Acoma and Zuñi territories, being more nearly related to the Mesa Verde type. So, also, were the glaze-paint red-ware series which immediately followed equally distinct from those typical for either Acoma or Zuñi. The glaze paint, in turn, gave way, as it did in the western towns, to a dull paint and apparently at about the same time.

---

* Sia, Cia, Zia and Tzia are also spellings that have been used but as these are all attempts to express the name phonetically, it has been found that the above spelling should have preference as best fitting the Indian pronunciation.

Designs, in many respects, tend to follow those of Acoma but incline to be more formal in character and possess a style which is not easily confused with anything from that village. Variations of the "Rain Bird" were and continue to be very popular and especially one arrangement, which, with individual interpretations, became what might almost be termed a stock design (Pls. XXXI, XXXII, XXXIII). It will also be noticed that although the bird idea is still in evidence, here and there an introduction of what appear to be floral forms has taken place.

SANTA ANA

A few miles below Tsia, in the same valley, lies the small pueblo of Santa Ana. Its language, and in many ways its material culture are very close to those of Tsia. Both have a like prehistoric background and it was not until the dull-paint wares of the historic period became established that a difference began to appear. Although pottery materials and general technique of the two are closely alike, there are marked differences in the handling of design. Broadly speaking, Santa Ana shows a lack of coherence and balance, judged by the average for Indian pottery decoration. A system utilizing simply conceived design units or elements broadly executed seems to be the rule and gives to the whole structure a feeling of heaviness. Among design formulae which express this over-solidity to the least degree are those based on the "Rain Bird" motif which may be seen to possess a measure of grace superior to the sorts more commonly employed (Pl. XXXV).

SAN ILDEFONSO

Heretofore the diffusion of a basic design has been traced with its many changes while passing from village to village in a west to east progress until it finally reached the valley of the Rio Grande. From this point instead of following what might otherwise be a normal spread up this valley, it will be necessary to reverse the order as a new pottery type, originating in the north, must first enter into the problem. The system of decoration used on this type greatly influenced the structure of design throughout this immediate region. Therefore a new start will be made beginning with San Ildefonso, the northernmost pueblo producing decorated pottery which included the "Rain Bird" motif in its decorative scheme. In order to understand the bearing that this pottery type, together with the system of design peculiar to it, has on the subject of this study, it is desirable that something of its prehistory should be known. Unlike the pottery of the western pueblos and that of some of its neighbors to the south, the wares ancestral to those of San Ildefonso were never affected by the great spread of glaze paint decoration which, in its day, dominated so large a part of the southwest. Instead, there was in this region an uninterrupted succession of pottery types based on Black-on-white wares which extended over a period of some seven hundred years. Throughout this sequence, designs were rigidly conventional and elementally geometric in character, consisting for the most part, if summed up, of combinations of lines in parallel arrangement or at various angles as a primary procedure with the corners or spaces between filled with solid figures. Dots, either between or appended to lines were much in evidence and hachure was used sparingly. There is little cause for wonder, that with such a rigidly formal heritage, when exuberance of design became the prevailing fashion, these people, speaking a totally different language (Tewa) as well, were at a loss how to follow the new trend, bound as they were by limits imposed by their unelastic system of design. The effort to keep abreast of the times usually resulted in badly conceived parodies and grotesque forms. Attempts to directly copy introduced designs display the best draughtsmanship but when these were adapted to conform to the prevailing style, the drawing was indifferent and shows but little comprehension of the idea for which they originally stood. Notwithstanding so poor a beginning it can be said that for the last two decades San Ildefonso potters, as decorators, occupy a position second to none (Pls. XXXVI-XL).

TESUQUE

The Pueblo of Tesuque, situated on a small stream of the same name, an eastern tributary of the Rio Grande, is distant about ten miles in a southeasterly direction from the village last discussed. The language spoken, like that of San Ildefonso, is Tewa. Its line of ceramic descent likewise belongs in the same category as that of the latter town. In fact, most of the statements made concerning San Ildefonso will apply equally to Tesuque up to the point when that wave of great elaboration of design swept over the Puebloan Southwest and became the vogue. At this period, instead of accomplishing a mere complexity by means of combining heterogeneous assortments of elements as was done by its more northern neighbor, Tesuque reached its objective by concentrating a great deal of attention on the smaller details of decoration. Units of design were very frequently bordered by rows of scallops, fringes, and serrations while many oddments including wavy lines were introduced. Despite an appearance of overdoing, there is, on the whole, more coherence shown than at San Ildefonso. In this latter pueblo the coil element derived from the "Rain Bird" still remained a prominent feature but here it becomes secondary in importance, often taking the form of a complete circle and serving principally as something upon which to attach elaborations of the design unit F which became the primary interest. Pottery designing in Tesuque reached its highest achievement some time before the close of the 19th Century, after which time a rapid decline set in with as yet no signs of a renaissance (Pls. XLI-XLIII).

COCHITI

Leaving the Tewa towns and proceeding southward, Keres territory is reentered at the pueblo of Cochiti, the northernmost settlement. Although the language spoken here belongs in the same group with that of Tsia and Santa Ana, the type of pottery made during a large part of the historic period, instead of following that of villages of the same linguistic affiliation, was derived from its Tewa speaking neighbors to the north. Thus there is seen an instance where a people, whose ceramic background included the normal use of glaze-paint wares up to the beginning of the 18th Century, borrowed an alien pottery type instead of attempting to invent or perpetuate some form based on the manner of their own tradition. This adopted type of pottery has been noted before as having inherited a very limited and elemental system of design expression. The result of attempts to utilize and conform to the Tewa system is very apparent on most examples of the older Cochiti pottery, and gives the impression of a struggle for effect without any understanding. There seems to be an almost total lack of formality in treatment, unrelated design entities being often scattered at random over the background. Neither the "Rain Bird" nor any of its components were much used and when employed were executed in a manner suggesting little comprehension of its original status. In justice to the present day potters of Cochiti, it should here be stated that within the last few years there has finally been developed a very distinctive and pleasing decorative art which is a direct and orderly outgrowth from an earlier heterogeneity (Pls. XLIV-XLV).

SANTO DOMINGO

Only five or six miles below Cochiti and on the opposite or east bank of the Rio Grande lies the large pueblo of Santo Domingo. Like the former village, it is a Keresan town. A further likeness also exists by reason that it too discarded its ceramic tradition for one borrowed from the Tewa. But unlike it or in fact any of the pueblos employing the Tewa formula, having once adopted that rather elemental system it proceeded, with a conservatism characteristic of this village, to make use of it in its simplest form, thus avoiding the later perflorid styles developed in the three northern towns just discussed. Hence the restraint and formality of Santo Domingo design is seen to be the result of the limits imposed by a strict adherence to that system, of which a brief outline has been previously given under the discussion of San Ildefonso. Although direct copies of "Rain Bird" forms on Santo Domingo pottery are known, the great majority of adaptations derived from that motif are mere attenuations of the original idea and were possibly employed as better conforming to the treatment demanded by the local type of decoration. It is quite noticeable, if designs which are obviously copies be not considered, that the coil element *A* became the principal concern and that the other normally accompanying elements have lost much of their identity and are only secondary in importance. Santo Domingo is the last of the pueblos to be here considered as being influenced by the design which in some form or other obtained so wide spread a popularity, and in no other town does it appear as frequently in so dilute a form (Pls. XLVI-XLVIII).

CONCLUSION

The number of designs figured on the accompanying plates could have been multiplied many times but it is believed that enough have been shown to demonstrate the relationship existing between those figured as well as to serve in pointing out their remote origin from a common source.

It must not be thought that the greater number of the many variations illustrated were necessarily direct adaptations of the original Zuñian concept but rather that most were the result of exchanges of the form idea between the several villages using the design together with such local alterations as might have been made from time to time.

Even a comparatively limited acquaintance with the general aspects of Pueblo culture will show that a great conservatism prevails throughout. To cite a striking instance, the ceremonial chamber of today, or kiva, as it is called, is merely a replica of a type of dwelling known to have been in common use some eleven hundred years ago and still survives in its newer capacity only by reason of an adherence to and veneration for things of the past. Likewise, though ceramic decoration demonstrates a slow but steady advance over a like period of time from simply conceived beginnings on through the years to a considerable degree of complexity, it is still possible to find at all stages of progression the continued use of unaltered elementary design structures. It is reasonable to suppose that this manifest conservatism reflects to a large degree a pattern of behavior—the result of having to cope with certain exigencies of existence in the past. At a period reckoned as some time during the early centuries of the Christian era when necessity is believed to have forced detached family groups to gather into communities for better cooperation and safety, there undoubtedly arose certain rules, compliance with which could alone assure the continued life of the group. Later, as these communities continued to grow in size, thus affording a still greater measure of protection, they must have become increasingly dependent on codes formulated in terms drastic enough to exercise control over the increasing population. Thus there would be devised a hard and fast set of organized regulations. So strong was the resulting organization, that affiliating peoples of whatever ethnic or linguistic stocks are seen to have been almost completely absorbed. That such a premise is tenable may be inferred from the fact that at the present time there are four unrelated languages as well as several distinct dialects spoken by Pueblo peoples all having in the main a similar system of government and culture. This would seem to indicate that although by weight of numbers alone some particular feature such as a language might have survived, yet the general cultural scheme into which these alien elements were introduced remained unaffected. Arts developed under these conditions would naturally reflect to a large extent the rigid conservatism of such a system and it is a notable fact that not even the advent of the conquering Spaniard and the later "Anglo" disturbed or influenced the aboriginal forms to any marked degree.

The brief outline just drawn of the conditions existing during prehistoric times is introduced here only to aid in an explanation of why pottery designs of the Southwest were confined within such definitely restricted bounds. This was so much the case that the artist was practically limited to modifications of the same units and elements over and over again and forced constantly to invent new combinations in order to produce different effects. Despite this apparent handicap the potter was able to produce pleasing and harmonious compositions. The evolution of the "Rain Bird" is but a single example of what could be accomplished within the limits of the traditional method and one which can be said to epitomize the general principles underlying the ceramic art of the Pueblos.

The writer believes that a regrettable ignorance, not only of the forms but of the laws governing the use of Pueblo design, is responsible for the neglect, as source material, of an art indigenous to our own country and that a study of this interesting subject will amply repay the modern designer by enabling him to inject a new note into future decorative schemes, at present dominated by themes originating in foreign lands.

BIBLIOGRAPHY

BUNZEL, RUTH L.;
    1929 The Pueblo potter, a study of creative imagination in primitive art. *Columbia University Contributions to Anthropology*, No. VIII. New York.

FEWKES, J. W.;
    1898 Archæological expedition to Arizona in 1895. *Seventeenth Report of the Bureau of American Ethnology*, pt. 2, pp. 519-742. Washington.

    1904 Two summers' work in pueblo ruins. *Twenty-second Report of the Bureau of American Ethnology*, pt. 1, pp. 3-195. Washington.

GLADWIN, WINIFRED and HAROLD S.;
    1931 Some Southwestern pottery types. Series II, *Medallion Papers*, No. X. Globe.

HARGRAVE, L. L.;
    1932 A guide to forty pottery types from the Hopi country and the San Francisco Mountains, Arizona. *Museum of Northern Arizona*, Bull. 1. Flagstaff.

HAURY, E. W. and HARGRAVE, L. L.;
    1931 Recently dated pueblo ruins in Arizona. *Smithsonian Miscellaneous Collections*, vol. 82, No. 11. Washington.

HOUGH, WALTER;
    1903 Archæological field-work in Northeastern Arizona, the Museum-Gates Expedition of 1901. *Annual Report of the U. S. National Museum for 1901*, pp. 279-358. Washington.

    1914 Culture of the ancient Pueblos of the upper Gila River region, New Mexico and Arizona. *U. S. National Museum*, Bull. 87. Washington.

KIDDER, A. V.;
    1924 An introduction to the study of Southwestern archæology with a preliminary account of the excavations at Pecos. *Papers of the Phillips Academy Southwestern Expedition*, No. 1. New Haven.

KIDDER, A. V. and AMSDEN, C. A.;
    1931 The pottery of Pecos, Vol. I, the dull paint wares. *Papers of the Phillips Academy Southwestern Expedition*, No. 5. New Haven.

NORDENSKIÖLD, G.;
    1893 The cliff-dwellers of the Mesa Verde. Translated by D. Lloyd Morgan. Stockholm.

PLATES

PLATE I

1. Sherd of late Basket Maker pottery showing little organization of design.
   Laboratory of Anthropology site $\frac{14}{530}$.

2. Early Pueblo pottery fragment with some degree of design organization and showing elongation of dots.
   Laboratory of Anthropology site $\frac{14}{1037}$.

3. Potsherd illustrating a fringe-like form of decoration on a time horizon nearly the same as that of 2 above.
   Laboratory of Anthropology site $\frac{14}{687}$.

4. Early example of angles filled solidly, the first stage in a departure from the simple line idea.
   Indian Arts Fund, 1604.

5. Hook-shaped elements from pottery fragment.
   Laboratory of Anthropology site $\frac{8}{571}$.

6. Sherd specimen showing an interlocking of two series of hook elements.
   Laboratory of Anthropology site $\frac{8}{1001}$.

1

2

3

4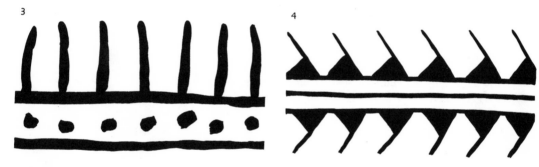

5

6

PLATE I

19

PLATE II

1-6. Various applications of the interlocking fret and coil idea. Examples 4 and 5 have the solid angle filling device (Pl. I, 4) embellished, while 6 shows this treatment applied to the coil elements. All were copied from sherds.

1. Laboratory of Anthropology site $\frac{14}{319}$.
2. Laboratory of Anthropology site $\frac{3}{1240}$.
3. Laboratory of Anthropology site $\frac{10}{376}$.
4. Laboratory of Anthropology site $\frac{8}{571}$.
5. Laboratory of Anthropology site $\frac{10}{1352}$.
6. Laboratory of Anthropology site $\frac{3}{503}$.

7. Hatching one and representing the other as solid differentiates these two opposing coil elements—a further development of the interlocking coil.

Laboratory of Anthropology site $\frac{10}{1352}$.

1

2

3

4

6

5

7

PLATE II

21

PLATE III

1. Typical interlocking fret pattern that is a conspicuous feature on Tularosa Black-on-white pottery.
   F. L. McCament Coll., 18.

2. The interlocking coil vied in popularity with the fret arrangement in Tularosa-type vessels.
   Laboratory of Anthropology site $\frac{2}{436}$.

1

2

PLATE III

PLATE IV

1-2. Interlocking coil designs that may represent steps in the evolution of certain bird forms.

    1. Laboratory of Anthropology 1368.

    2. After Hough, 1914, p. 48, fig. 87.

  3. Graphic bird design which still retains features of interlocking coil.
After Kidder, 1931, p. 69, fig. g.

4-5. Bird forms taken from Mesa Verde Black-on-white pottery.

    4. After Nordenskiöld, 1893, Pl. XXVIII, fig. 3.

    5. After Kidder, 1924, p. 63, fig. d.

6-7. Forms occurring on Jeddito Black-on-yellow wares. Number 6 used on bowl exterior. Number 7 used in bowl interior.

    6. Indian Arts Fund 622.

    7. Indian Arts Fund 622.

8-9. Forms found on Four-mile Polychrome pottery. Used on bowl exteriors only.
After Haury, 1931, p. 68, figs. b, g.

PLATE IV

PLATE V

1-4. Typical Four-mile Polychrome bowl decoration. Note that only a single decorated coil element is here used depending from an elaborately designed area, the appearance of an opposing coil being simulated by the plain bowl background.

1. Mus. of the Univ. of Pennsylvania 29-77-680.
2-3. After Fewkes, 1904, Pl. XXIX, fig. b; Pl. XL, fig. a.
4. Laboratory of Anthropology $\frac{30}{895}$.

1

3   4

2

PLATE V

27

PLATE VI

SIKYATKI POLYCHROME BOWL DESIGNS

The single coil is a prominent feature and is utilized as part of an abstract bird motif.

1. After Hough, 1903, Pl. 98, lower
2. After Fewkes, 1898, Pl. CL, fig. c.

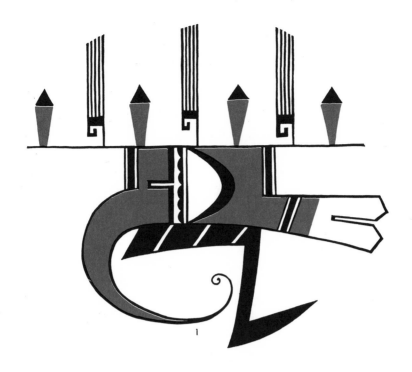

PLATE VI

PLATE VII

1. Typical form of Zuñi "Rain Bird."
   Letters *A, B, C* and *D* show relationship with certain features of Tularosa designs shown below (2-3). The single coil motif is believed to have been derived directly from Sikyatki Polychrome and indirectly from Tularosa Black-on-white by way of Four-mile Polychrome.
   Indian Arts Fund 3.

2-3. Tularosa Black-on-White pottery designs.
   Refer to Plate III.

4. A variation of the "Rain Bird" pattern with the coil omitted and a new element *E* introduced.
   Indian Arts Fund 412.

PLATE VII

PLATE VIII

Two examples showing alteration and a breaking down of the original concept.

1. Note omission of unit C (see Plate VII).
   Indian Arts Fund 1877.

2. A much altered adaptation and the introduction of a new design unit F which later becomes of great importance. Although only a single B element has been used the C is retained but out of the usual position on the coil.
   Indian Arts Fund 4.

2

PLATE VIII

PLATE IX

Examples of hatched and partially hatched coils which comprise one of three divisions into which all derivations of the "Rain Bird" pattern may be divided.

Numbers 1, 2, and 3 retain element C. B is also present but exceeds the usual number by one.

Numbers 1 and 3 exhibit E (Pl. VII).

Number 4 has lost all its appendages but a trace of F (Pl. VIII).

1. Indian Arts Fund 3.
2. Indian Arts Fund 1290.
3. Indian Arts Fund 1291.
4. Indian Arts Fund 1364.

PLATE IX

35

PLATE X

Various forms based on the hatched coil.

Numbers 1 and 3 show use of *E* and 1 retains *D* (Pl. VII).

Numbers 4 and 5 form a continuous band.

1. Indian Arts Fund 860.
2. Indian Arts Fund 1514.
3. Indian Arts Fund 611.
4. Indian Arts Fund 1877.
5. Indian Arts Fund 1023.

1

2

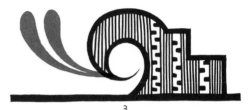

3

4

5

PLATE X

PLATE XI

SOME UNUSUAL DERIVATIONS

1-2. show the coil as secondary in importance to the F unit.

3. has the B-C arrangement of the old Tularosa design above a part of the coil (Plate VII).

4. also uses three B elements and an altered tripartite C horizontally.

5. can claim relationship only through general features.

    1. Indian Arts Fund 543.
    2. Indian Arts Fund 392.
    3. Indian Arts Fund 858.
    4. Indian Arts Fund 977.
    5. Indian Arts Fund 512.

1

2

3

4

5

PLATE XI

PLATE XII

Diagrams to explain the evolution of the F design unit into a form which was most frequently used and widely borrowed—a group that constitutes the second division of "Rain Bird" derivations.

The letters are used in the same relations as those in Plates VII and VIII.

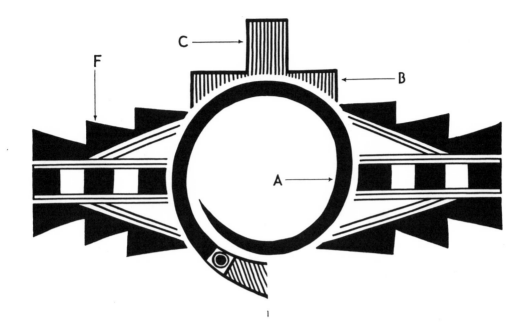

1

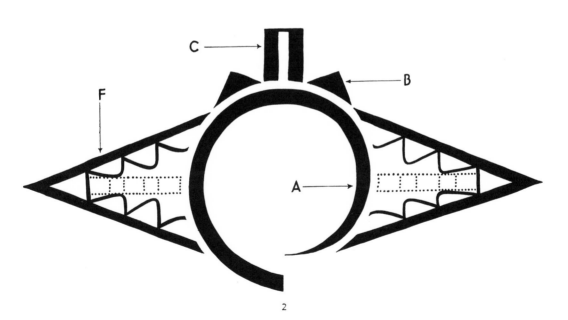

2

PLATE XII

PLATE XIII

Examples classed as belonging in second division of "Rain Bird" derivatives. Compare 2 on this plate with the diagrams on Plate XII. The *C* element is seldom used in this division.

1. Indian Arts Fund 8.
2. Indian Arts Fund 851.
3. Indian Arts Fund 6.
4. Indian Arts Fund 1365.
5. Indian Arts Fund 1346.

PLATE XIII

PLATE XIV

More examples of second division designs. The coil has been distorted to enclose an oval space in 3 and forms a closed ring in 4.

1. Indian Arts Fund 775.
2. Indian Arts Fund 393.
3. Indian Arts Fund 1988.
4. Indian Arts Fund 859.

2

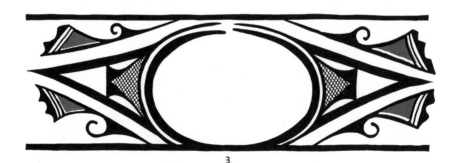

3

4

Plate XIV

45

PLATE XV

Another lot of second division examples. Number 4 is part of a running pattern which completely encircles the jar.

1. Indian Arts Fund 952
2. Indian Arts Fund 859.
3. Indian Arts Fund 182.
4. Indian Arts Fund 798.

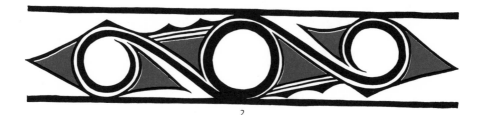

1

3

4

Plate XV

47

PLATE XVI

Group of simplified forms probably derived from the second division and to be classed in a distinct group as division three. Note the use of this symbol as a head for a dragonfly (10) and as a bird's tail (9). Number 10 was copied from a ceremonial vessel.

1. Indian Arts Fund 949.
2. Indian Arts Fund 1432.
3. Indian Arts Fund 251.
4. Indian Arts Fund 10.
5. Indian Arts Fund 318.
6. Indian Arts Fund 782.
7. Indian Arts Fund 229.
8. Indian Arts Fund 170.
9. Indian Arts Fund 189.
10. Indian Arts Fund 1273.
11. Indian Arts Fund 1359.

PLATE XVI

PLATE XVII

HOPI ADAPTATIONS

In all of these the coil and F units are most prominent. B elements are not present on 1 but are employed on both 2 and 3. Note a hatched B-C combination used independently at either end of panel enclosing design 3. (Refer to Plates VII and VIII).

1. Indian Arts Fund 1690.
2. Indian Arts Fund 743.
3. Indian Arts Fund 116.

1

2

3

PLATE XVII

PLATE XVIII

HOPI ADAPTATIONS (*Continued*)

Element *B* is missing in 1 and 4 (Refer to Plate VII).

1. Indian Arts Fund 409.
2. Indian Arts Fund 506.
3. Indian Arts Fund 403.
4. Indian Arts Fund 408.

1

2

3

4

PLATE XVIII

PLATE XIX

Hopi Adaptations (*Continued*)

In 2 a circle has replaced the coil element; 4 has been derived from the third division of Zuñian forms (Refer to Plate XVI).

1. Indian Arts Fund 634.
2. Indian Arts Fund 468.
3. J. L. Nelson Coll.
4. Indian Arts Fund 713.

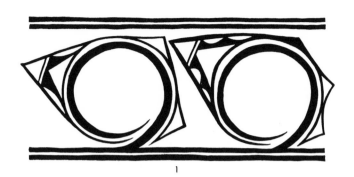

1

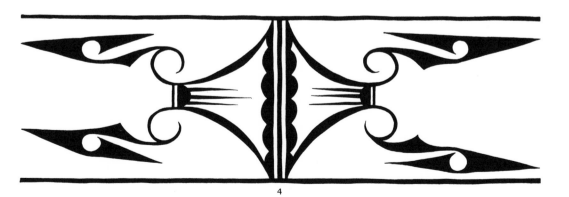

2

3

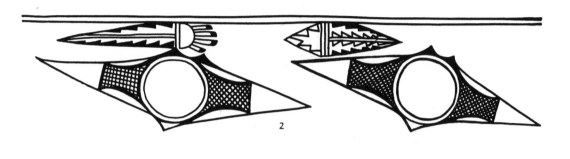

4

Plate XIX

PLATE XX

Hopi Adaptations (*Continued*)

Number 1 has been taken from Zuñi first division or hatched coil group (Refer to Plates IX and X). Much altered derivatives are shown in 2 and 3. In 2, single B elements are used in place over each coil and a solid B-C combination will be found between. The coil is related to the hatched variety. Number 3 is a much altered form with element B in red below the coil which is tipped by elements taken from a Zuñi third division form. Attention is called to the four B-C combinations two of which are hatched, the others being solid black.

1. Indian Arts Fund 41.
2. Indian Arts Fund 118.
3. Indian Arts Fund 407.

1

2

3

PLATE XX

PLATE XXI

Acoma Forms

The central design 2 shows the nearest resemblance to the Zuñi type but generally Acoma expressed the motif in her own terms. In 1 the more recognizable *F* unit seen placed on the outer circumference of the coil is replaced near the top of the coil by a stepped figure.

Instead of being placed normally, a *C* element has been introduced within the coil in 2 while in 3 this feature has been used to attach the design to a base line. Attention is also called to two rounded *B* elements on either side of *C*. (Refer to Plate XII).

1. Indian Arts Fund 1028.
2. Indian Arts Fund 1497.
3. Indian Arts Fund 1446.

2

3

PLATE XXI

PLATE XXII

This plate shows variations of the use of *F* unit, both the more normal sort as well as the stepped variety, the latter being an Acoman development; 5 is a running design.

1. Indian Arts Fund 1675.
2. Indian Arts Fund 936.
3. Indian Arts Fund 1575.
4. Indian Arts Fund 1583.
5. Indian Arts Fund 1079.

1

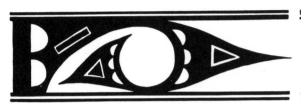

2

3

4

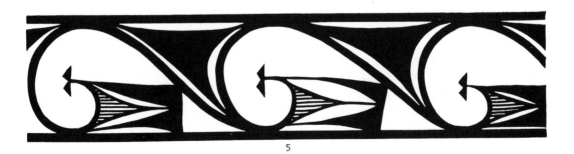

5

PLATE XXII

PLATE XXIII

Two B elements will be noted near the distal end of each coil and the usual F unit has been placed near its top in the topmost figure; 2 and 3 have only made use of the coil and F unit which is represented in 3 by a hatched stepped form. No C elements appear.

1. Indian Arts Fund 1049.
2. Indian Arts Fund 795.
3. Indian Arts Fund 1075.

1

2

3

PLATE XXIII

PLATE XXIV

Both 1 and 3 show only the use of the coil and F units, the latter being of the stepped variety; 2 has in addition a C element in normal position.

1. Indian Arts Fund 645.
2. Indian Arts Fund 1036.
3. Indian Arts Fund 1687.

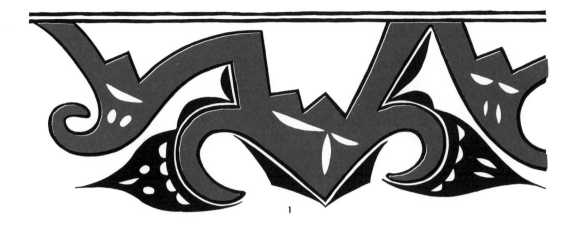

1

2

3

PLATE XXIV

PLATE XXV

Number 3 shows an *F* unit reminiscent of certain Zuñi types. In 2 will be noticed in addition to a hatched *F* unit attached near the tip of the coil, a simplified solid form of the same on the outer circumference. A figure based on the hatched stepped idea may be seen in 1.

1. Indian Arts Fund 180.
2. Indian Arts Fund 326.
3. Indian Arts Fund 1150.

1

2

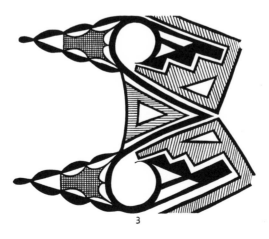

3

PLATE XXV

PLATE XXVI

LATER AND MORE DECADENT FORMS (*Continued*)

Number 1 is a running design and 2 a panel in which only the coil and modification of the *F* unit are used. Number 3 shows a similar usage but is part of an all-over pattern in which these features are almost lost in the general mass.

1. Indian Arts Fund 1125.
2. Indian Arts Fund 1096.
3. Indian Arts Fund 1099.

1

2

3

PLATE XXVI

PLATE XXVII

Unusual Acoman Forms

Number 1 demonstrates considerable outside influence, either late Hopi or Zuñi (Refer to Pl. XI). In 2 relationships have become very obscure but besides the coils four examples of element *C* may be seen out of place (Refer to Pl. XII). Number 3 shows little definitely identifiable but the coil.

1. Indian Arts Fund 1120.
2. Indian Arts Fund 227.
3. Indian Arts Fund 960.

2

3

PLATE XXVII

71

PLATE XXVIII

Laguna forms are very similar to those of Acoma and will need no comment.

1. Indian Arts Fund 1026.
2. Indian Arts Fund 792.

1

2

Plate XXVIII

73

PLATE XXIX

Three Early Historic Tsia Designs

1. Three *F* units are attached to the coil in the topmost example.
   Indian Arts Fund 84.

2. This pattern presents the *B* and *C* elements in a normal situation in relation to the coil. Four *F* units may be seen projecting to the left.
   Indian Arts Fund 1486.

3. Here the four *B* elements take a loop-like form around the circumference of the coil.
   Indian Arts Fund 666.

2

3

PLATE XXIX

PLATE XXX

Tsia Derivations

In the three examples figured only the coil and F unit appear. The coils of the top and bottom designs enclose a vegetal motif while that of the center contains a bird form. Either one or the other of these two types almost invariably occupies this position. In 2 the F unit has been placed in a vertical position.

1. Indian Arts Fund 516.
2. Indian Arts Fund 840.
3. Indian Arts Fund 497.

1

2

3

PLATE XXX

PLATE XXXI

Three examples of a type of design with many variations, very popular at Tsia.

1. Only coils and F units are used.
   Indian Arts Fund 120.

2. This example utilizes a number of altered B elements with the coil instead of the more usual F unit.
   Indian Arts Fund 604.

3. Besides the coils and F units, a C element is used to attach the former to top and bottom lines.
   Indian Arts Fund 633.

2

3

PLATE XXXI

PLATE XXXII

Top and bottom examples make use of coils and F units. This latter has been omitted from the central design and is replaced by a number of elements B and C (Refer to Pl. XII). In 1 a divided circular figure attaches the left hand coil to the border line above; in 2 this function is accomplished by means of a divided lozenge both above and below. These may have been derived from a C element.

1. Indian Arts Fund 235.
2. Indian Arts Fund 573.
3. Indian Arts Fund 663.

1

2

3

PLATE XXXII

PLATE XXXIII

TSIA DERIVATIONS (*Continued*)

The two lower designs belong to the group typified by those on the two previous plates. In 2 may be seen a divided circular figure that attaches the coil to top and base lines which may have been derived from an element C, a feature already mentioned for 1 and 2, Plate XXXII. No attached F unit appears in 3 but the F units are used as an independent feature. Note that the B elements in this example have been changed into a scalloped arc.

1. Indian Arts Fund 784.
2. Indian Arts Fund 360.
3. Indian Arts Fund 364.

1

2

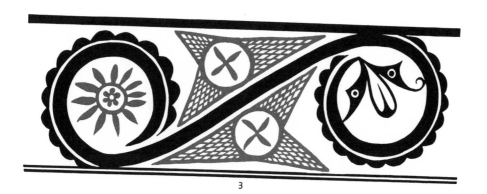

3

PLATE XXXIII

PLATE XXXIV

Unusual Tsia Adaptations

All derivatives shown here except those in the lower figure are simplified forms of the usual coil and F unit type but those in 3 have been plainly taken from some form in the Zuñian third division (Refer to Plate XVI).

1. Binkley Coll.
2. Indian Arts Fund 968.
3. Indian Arts Fund 1397.

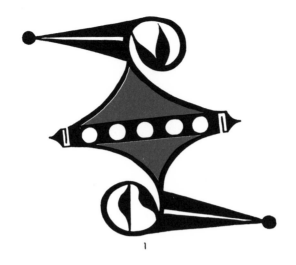

1

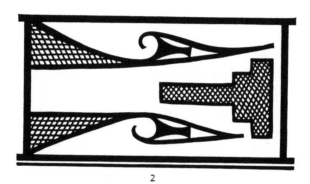

2

3

PLATE XXXIV

PLATE XXXV

SANTA ANA ADAPTATIONS

1-2. In these the coils, F units and C elements are conventionally placed (Refer to Plate XII).
Indian Arts Fund 874.
Indian Arts Fund 129.

3. The coil is here done in red and is represented as pierced by two irregularly shaped openings. Three F units are appended and one is used independently.
Spanish and Indian Trading Co. Coll.

4. This design shows no coil—F units alone are the principal feature.
Indian Arts Fund 479.

2

3

4

PLATE XXXV

87

PLATE XXXVI

SAN ILDEFONSO FORMS

1. This shows strong evidence of being partially copied but otherwise adapted from an Acoman original. Note typical solid stepped unit at either end of design. American Museum of Natural History $\frac{50.1}{3269}$.

2. Shows, in addition to coil and F units, a number of Zuñi third division symbols. Indian Arts Fund 64.

3. Besides the coils this drawing displays five poorly conceived F units—three on the left side and two on the right. Indian Arts Fund 556.

1

2

3

PLATE XXXVI

89

PLATE XXXVII

San Ildefonso Forms (*Continued*)

Number 1 is the only design on the plate to show an attempt to copy a conventional form, design unit *F*. A series of serrate forms paralleling the coil outline was derived from either an *F* unit, a *B* element or a little of both.

1. American Museum of Natural History 33740.
2. Indian Arts Fund 510.
3. Indian Arts Fund 593.

1

2

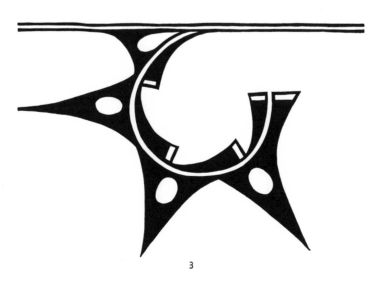

3

PLATE XXXVII

PLATE XXXVIII

San Ildefonso Forms on Pottery of More Recent Years

1. Shows coil with a simplified *F* unit attached.
   Indian Arts Fund 585.

2. Note that the coil has been converted into an inverted U to which two *F* units
   are appended on either side.
   Indian Arts Fund 583.

3. In this example the *F* units have been greatly elaborated and in no way resemble
   the prototype.
   Indian Arts Fund 585.

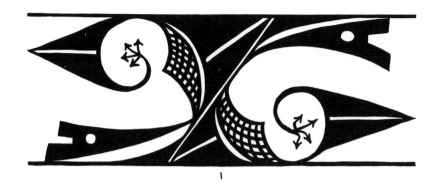

1

2

3

PLATE XXXVIII

93

PLATE XXXIX

SAN ILDEFONSO FORMS

Number 1 shows appendages attached to the coil that were derived from either *F* units, *B* elements or both. Symbols adopted from Zuñi division three forms may be seen on 2 and 3 (Refer to Plate XVI).

1. Indian Arts Fund 192.
2. Indian Arts Fund 616.
3. Indian Arts Fund 525.

1

2

3

PLATE XXXIX

PLATE XL

SAN ILDEFONSO FORMS (*Continued*)

1 and 3 illustrate varieties with serrations derived from a coil with its more conventional accompaniments and 2 is another example of a Zuñi third division symbol (Refer to Plate XVI).

1. Indian Arts Fund 217.
2. Indian Arts Fund 525.
3. Indian Arts Fund 761.

1

2

3

PLATE XL

PLATE XLI

1. The coil here assumes the form of a circle to which are appended four F design units (Refer to Plate XII).
   Indian Arts Fund 809.

2. This design comes nearer the normal convention. F units and B elements are clearly seen.
   Indian Arts Fund 1921.

3. There is a strong Acoman influence evident but the circle instead of the coil would hardly have been used at that village. The two serrate features are strongly Acoman.
   Indian Arts Fund 586.

1

2

3

PLATE XLI

99

PLATE XLII

Tesuque Adaptations (*Continued*)

In this group closed circles or ovals replace the coil. All three show the use of unit F but in addition 1 plainly displays an example of an elaborate element C with two B elements in place on either side.

1. Indian Arts Fund 1921.
2. Indian Arts Fund 809.
3. Indian Arts Fund 824.

1

2

3

PLATE XLII

PLATE XLIII

Tesuque Adaptations (*Continued*)

1. In this example the coil or even the circle idea has been abandoned for a figure which may be a floral outline, but the positions of what stand for two F units are retained.
Indian Arts Fund 731.

2. Again a circle is substituted for the coil to which are attached two F units in a vertical position. An unusual feature is the addition to the design of four D units (Refer to Plate VII).
Indian Arts Fund 843.

3. Here the coil and F unit idea is quite clear.
Indian Arts Fund 993.

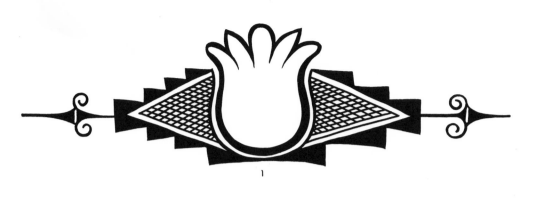

1

2

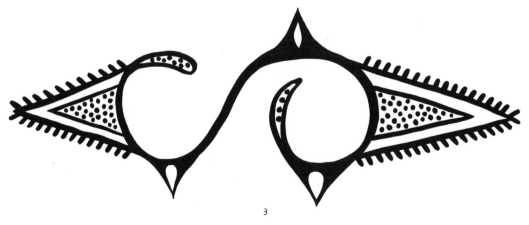

3

PLATE XLIII

PLATE XLIV

In figures 1 and 2 the detection of both coil and F units offers no difficulty. A series of serrate forms paralleling the coil outline was derived from either unit F, B elements or a little of both.

1. Indian Arts Fund 876.
2. Indian Arts Fund 379.
3. Indian Arts Fund 244.

1

2

3

PLATE XLIV

PLATE XLV

COCHITI FORMS (*Continued*)

1. A running pattern composed of coils and solid *F* units.
   Indian Arts Fund 301.

2. The coil with attached dotted *F* units is surmounted by the figure of a turkey.
   Indian Arts Fund 272.

3. Note the use of the Zuñian third division symbols (Refer to Plate XVI).
   Indian Arts Fund 434.

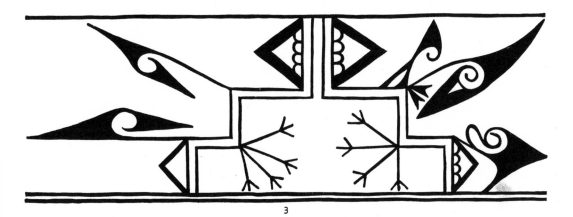

PLATE XLV

PLATE XLVI

Santo Domingo Derivations

1. A conventional treatment of the coil and F appendages is shown.
   Indian Arts Fund 538.

2. In addition to the coil and the three hatched F units there are also two B elements which are rounded instead of being angled.
   Indian Arts Fund 1419.

3. Crudely executed coil and F unit design.

PLATE XLVI

PLATE XLVII

SANTO DOMINGO DERIVATIONS (*Continued*)

Only one of these examples (3) shows the use of the F unit but all surround the coil element with a connected row of B elements as a principal feature.

1. Indian Arts Fund 728.
2. Indian Arts Fund 340.
3. Indian Arts Fund 82.

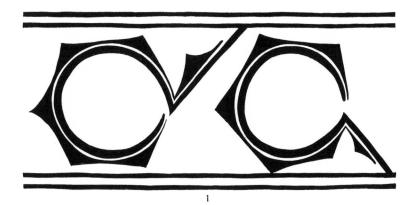

1

2

3

PLATE XLVII

PLATE XLVIII

Santo Domingo Forms

Numbers 1 and 3 demonstrate further forms of the coil and accompanying series of serrations derived from element B. Number 2 is an aberrant form undoubtedly being an attempt to copy from an Acoman source. The attachments for an abortive unit F may be seen as a series of arched openings on the right and left of the two outside coil elements. Compare these openings with those connecting an Acoman unit F to its coil on Plate XXI, 1.

1. Spanish and Indian Trading Co. Coll.
2. Indian Arts Fund 533.
3. Indian Arts Fund 493.

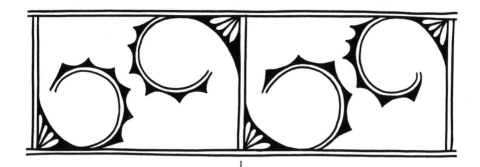

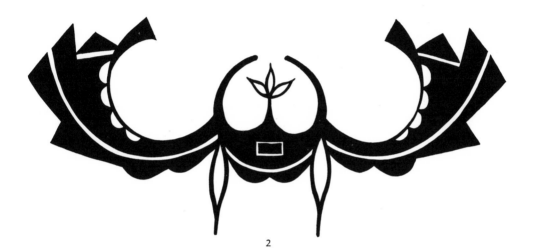

1

2

3

PLATE XLVIII

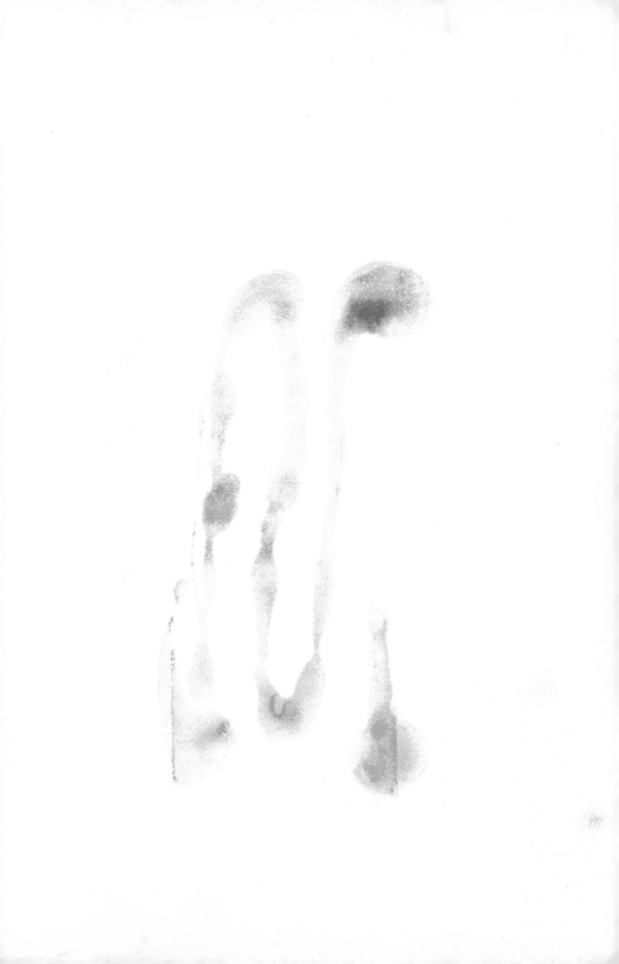

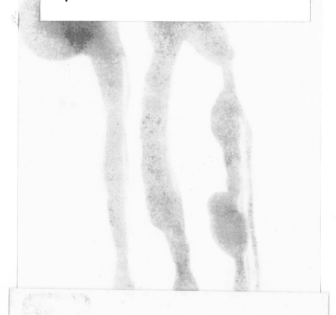